D0411631

As Far As I Know

As Far As I Know

Roger McGough

VIKING
an imprint of
PENGUIN BOOKS

VIKING

Published by the Penguin Group
Penguin Books Ltd, 80 Strand, London WC2R ORL, England
Penguin Group (USA) Inc., 375 Hudson Street, New York, New York 10014, USA
Penguin Group (Canada), 90 Eglinton Avenue East, Suite 700, Toronto, Ontario, Canada M4P 2Y3
(a division of Pearson Penguin Canada Inc.)
Penguin Ireland, 25 St Stephen's Green, Dublin 2, Ireland (a division of Penguin Books Ltd)
Penguin Group (Australia), 250 Camberwell Road, Camberwell, Victoria 3124, Australia
(a division of Pearson Australia Group Pty Ltd)
Penguin Books India Pvt Ltd, 11 Community Centre, Panchsheel Park, New Delhi – 110 017, India
Penguin Group (NZ), 67 Apollo Drive, Rosedale, Auckland 0632, New Zealand
(a division of Pearson New Zealand Ltd)
Penguin Books (South Africa) (Pty) Ltd, Block D, Rosebank Office Park, 181 Jan Smuts Avenue,
Parktown North, Gauteng 2193, South Africa

Penguin Books Ltd, Registered Offices: 80 Strand, London WC2R ORL, England

www.penguin.com

First published 2012
001

Copyright © Roger McGough, 2012

The moral right of the author has been asserted

Set in 12.5/15 pt Dante MT Std
Typeset by Jouve (UK), Milton Keynes
Printed in Great Britain by Clays Ltd, St Ives plc

A CIP catalogue record for this book is available from the British Library

ISBN: 978-0-670-92174-4

www.greenpenguin.co.uk

MIX
Paper from
responsible sources
FSC
www.fsc.org   FSC™ C018179

ALWAYS LEARNING

For Hilary

Contents

Take Comfort

Take comfort from this.
You have a book in your hand
not a loaded gun or a parking fine
or an invitation card to the wedding
of the one you should have married
but were too selfish. Always imagining
there would be someone better out there
but there wasn't, and you missed the boat.
And now you're pushing forty, what are the chances
of your finding that perfect elusive partner? Highly unlikely.
Like an empty glass on a bar-room counter, loneliness beckons.

Not an empty glass, or a bottle smashed on a bar-room counter
a photograph of the one you will always regret not marrying
not a letter from the hospital, the results devastating.
After the disaster, the dust and the screaming
a child's arm thrust out from the rubble.
You have none of these in your hand.
A dirty syringe or a deadly scorpion
a Molotov cocktail or an overdose
not a loaded gun or a parking fine
you have a book in your hand.
Take comfort from this.

Another Time, Another Place

Another Time

A summer's day on the beach at Seaforth.
There is a war on, so sunshine is rationed, and the sea
half a mile away, never more than a wet promise.
Unmanned pill-boxes gaze sullenly out over the Mersey.
Rotting dragon's teeth, half submerged, wait to repel
enemy tanks. Crabs scuttle across minefields.

A three-year-old follows the ball
as it bounces over the wire
and skims across the sand,
windswept, light as a balloon.

A girl still in her teens
finds the gap in the barbed wire
and races after him.
Scoops him up and bursts into tears.

The area had been cordoned off
and the MOD signs made clear the danger.
But little boys can't read
and balls are there for the chasing.

Another Place

A summer's day with Aunty Kath on the beach at Crosby,
where a platoon of Gormley's iron men are now stationed.
Has she any recollection of running across a minefield
to rescue me all those years ago? Or is my imagination
playing tricks? A scene perhaps from a film half recalled?

'All true,' she says. 'You gave us the fright of our lives
running off like that.' 'It was the big red rubber ball,'
I said. 'I remember chasing after it in the wind.'
My aunt stopped. 'Red rubber ball? There was no ball.
You were following the dog. You remember Goldie?'

A golden retriever finds a gap in the barbed wire
and races across the sand. Suddenly an explosion.
The dog obliterated in one ear-splitting instant.
The child turned into an iron statue. Eyes tightly shut
he watches the red ball bounce harmlessly into the distance.

To Sentimentality

I always warmed to the sound of you
The rhyme of you. But in times like these,
hardened and fearful, you are mistrusted.
A small-town Mantovani of the emotions.

Born nostalgic, and burdened with empathy
I would be told off by my parents
for wanting to be an orphan. Poor old Joe,
Out in the cold, cold snow

Nowhere to wonder, nowhere to go.
There but for the grace. Cue cheap music.
You have been my reality over the years
Sentimentality, the smile on the verge of tears.

    ★ ★ ★

Tears for the father giving away the bride
Tears for the snowman in the rain outside
Two Cs and a D and I'm bursting with pride

Any national anthem will stir my soul
Chips and Tizer, toad-in-the-hole
O those riverbank days with Ratty and Mole

The mission at Rorke's Drift under attack
Zola Budd's collision on the Olympic track
Bambi's mother, come back, come back!

To every loser I award a prize
I feel for the bees and the butterflies
The word *endangered* brings tears to my eyes

Lisdoonvarna and Innisfree
The mountains of Mourne, the Rose of Tralee
Not sure where they are, but they're heaven to me

Small dogs and kittens don't have to be cute
A schoolgirl embarrassing us all on the flute
The accused in a borrowed, ill-fitting suit

A lock of hair, lovers sighing
A stopped clock, babies crying,
Anyone, anywhere, giving birth or dying

    ★ ★ ★

Nearing the end of the poem
and already I feel your presence in the room
A sweet enveloping sadness

Nostalgia for those innocent times
of confident first lines and clear mornings.
The smell of coffee, an empty page.

Pakoras

You remember coal being delivered by horse and cart, surely?
And your mother made you watch from the backyard window
And count how many bags the coalie humped into the shed?
(Otherwise he'd cheat, throw down an empty one.)
And sarsaparilla came in refillable earthenware jars?
You remember that, surely?

Don't worry, this will not be a list poem writ in sepia.
No threepenny joeys, dolly tubs or ration books
No trams, no fog, no Carmen Miranda. This is memory,
Real as the pakoras at yesterday's buffet lunch.

Window-gazing

Funeral director's window
This is a headstone.
That's an urn. Job done.
No spring offers. No clearance sales

Butcher's window
The friendly face
of the abattoir

Haberdasher's window
Pulling our eyes
over the wool

Windows of the soul
The eyes have it

Prison windows
Imprisoned all day
Light waits for lights-out
in order to escape

Window-factory windows
Cheap to make
Easy to break
Quick to replace

Empty shop windows
We live in hope for weeks
and then,
another bloody estate agent's

Window-shopping
Went window-shopping
Bought a sash, two casements
and a uPVC tilt & turn

Sex-shop window
Don't look
You might see your reflection
wearing a basque and suspenders

Window of opportunity
'You look lovely in black
Sorry to hear about Sam.'

Widow of opportunity
'Don't be sorry
Our marriage was a sham.'

One-pound-shop shop window
'Here's 50p.
Can I have half a window, please.'

Jewellery-shop window
'I smash, you grab.
Lenny, you clean up afterwards
We don't want broken glass all over the pavement.'

Betting-shop window
Two flies land simultaneously
on a Grand National poster and start climbing.
'Twenty quid, the one on the right.'

Book-shop window
Where's mine? Where's mine?

Magic-shop window
Now you see it . . .

Psychopath window
Who are you looking at?

Fishmonger's window
Beneath the brill and the bream
the scallops and haddock
the shrimp and mackerel,
a mermaid's comb

Old-folks'-home window
A familiar face
Someone beckoning
Time. If only there were more time

City Lights bookshop window
Ferlinghetti recalls with a certain fondness
the day Corso, stoned and angry,
hurled a till through the plate glass

Greek-café window
Today's special—
Moussaka, chips and salad

Rose-tinted café window
Today's special—
So is every day

Lovers' bedroom window
Peepingtom moon
Better close the curtains

Fenêtre d'atelier de René Magritte
Ceci n'est pas une fenêtre

Windsor Castle window
King George VI and family gazing vacantly out
as Mr Eliot reads passages from *The Waste Land*

Taxidermist's window
Is that his wife?
She's been sitting still
for an awfully long time

Picture-framer's window
A wide selection of frames
perfectly framed

Cop-shop window
What do you mean, it's been stolen?

Shoe-shop window
Shoes mainly

Boarded-up windows
Blindfolded, dreading the wail
of police sirens

★

★★

**The
tallest
building
in the
world
(so far)
window**

★★★

★★★★

From the
ozymandias
observation
platform
way up
on the
hundred
and twenty
fourth floor
the visitor
on a clear day
can see the lone
and level sands
stretch far away

★★★★★★★★★★★★★★

★★★★★★★★★★★★★★

The Wallet

(A poem for three voices)

The Young Man

In Edinburgh at the height of the Festival
a young lady tosses herself into the torrent
of tourists crossing on green, and in so doing
drops her wallet.

Treading water, I see it on the pavement
and caught for an instant in the rigor of indecision,
watch both disappear. The girl into the crowd
and the wallet

into the shoulder bag of a woman heading
in the opposite direction. Scooped up
with barefaced nonchalance by her partner.
I follow them.

Perhaps they are looking for the owner?
Perhaps they are looking for a policeman?
Perhaps they are performing a surreal piece
of street theatre?

They turn suddenly and confront me.
I gesture dumbly to where the wallet had been,
and to where it now was. She mimes zipping a lip,
he, slitting a throat.

I mime having a photographic memory
and being a close friend of DI John Rebus,
before disappearing into the crowd,
crushed with shame.

Meanwhile, at the foot of the Mound,
a girl in tears is swimming upriver
towards Princes Street, her heart flapping
like a landed salmon.

The Hard Man

Saturday afternoon an Tina an me are fightin our way
through the crowds on Princes Street
when this lassie drops a wallet.
Finders keepers, nae bother.

Then sum numpty tries to gie us grief
Aw bletherin an twitchin
Sae Tina gie im *Hauld yer wheest*,
and I gie im *Or you're fuckin deid*

While he pisses himself we swerve doon Grassmarket
tae celebrate. Get blootered an score some johnny

Next thing Tina takes the wallet tae the bog
An d'ye ken? It wis empty nae cash nae cards
nae naethin. Ah dinnae believe it
Aw that trouble fer fuck aw.

The Young Lady

What you do is choose a busy café
buy a bowl of soup, sit in a corner
and pretend to read a Fringe brochure.

In no time someone's chatting away
and there's a handbag under the table
or on the bench next to you.

Or some guy will think he's on
'A coffee? Aye, that'll be great.'
BlackBerry on the table, car keys maybe.

This morning a wallet. My lucky day.

On Reigate Hill

On Reigate Hill this mild March day
winter's chill seems far away. Newly sprung,
daffodils flaunt their glowing effervescence.
From a distant lawn, the whirr of a new mower
in the air, a whiff of posh manure.

Below, the little town goes about its business.
From the escarpment to the west, a hang-glider
dives in at the deep end. Suddenly, a frenzied peal
of church bells, as steeples sway and topple
and birds are shaken from the trees.

As the horizon tilts and blurs, I am thrown down
by a violent vibration, and sense the terrible anger
of the earth beneath threatening to explode.
Slowly the fury subsides into muffled sobs.
Steeples reassert themselves.

Then stillness. The hang-glider comes up for air.
How can people go on living here? Putting up with
tremors and aftershocks? Live their lives indifferent
to disaster, to earthquake, tsunami and radiation?
Don't they watch television? Read the newspapers?

I am halfway down the path when the volcano erupts.
A Vesuvian fountain of fire and burning ash.
Two girls riding by on ponies smile. Rainbows
of reassurance. The scalding steam evaporates
and the molten lava flows back up the hillside.

On reaching the road, a shadow blots out the sun
and a wind like no other screams through the valley.
Three-legged hikers file past laughing and talking.
Behind them, Reigate Hill, above them, an asteroid
the size of an oil tanker singles out Dorking.

They Came out Singing

They came out singing.
Carapaced in dust, broken bodies
Pulled from broken buildings.
Days of sepulchral darkness,
Nights choked with disbelief.
First the smile, Lazarus risen,
Thanking God for his mercy.
Then the song, merci, merci.

Defence

(After Philip Larkin's 'Homage to a Government', 1969)

It takes money and patience to keep the peace
And we are running out of both
So we are bringing our soldiers home

They risked their lives, every one of them
To subdue an enemy they didn't hate
But now they are coming home

Who sent them there, or why,
Few of us remember, but the country
Will never forget the sacrifices they made

It is called defence, and defence costs money
But money is short, and the concern
Is that people here may take to the streets

There is a growing sense of panic
The government can no longer control
With promises and reassuring words

Let the enemy, unsubdued and far away
Find other enemies to fight against
For England has worries of its own

It will be done quietly and without fuss
We are running out of money
So we are bringing our soldiers home.

The Cat in Me

Gazing out as snowflakes continue to fall

The child in me sees the icing on the cake
where the lawn used to be
Wants my footprints to be first on the path
My snowman to be the one who comes to life

The man in me wonders when it will end
Will the flurry become a storm?
Are the pavements safe to negotiate?
Will the central-heating boiler cope?

The father in me worries about the daughter
in her cold student flat
huddled beneath unfinished canvases
frenzied gulls stabbing at the window

The cat in me
stretches and settles in front of the fire.

Die Barriere

Leaving the Common we walk down roads
unfamiliar to us. Left or right? It doesn't matter,
home is only fifteen minutes away.

You finish college in a few months and talk of spending
a year abroad. Not the Far East, not America,
you'd prefer Europe, and I'm thankful.

Berlin appeals. 'If I spoke German I could easily
find work in a bar.' I stop myself suggesting
she would pick it up soon enough.

Let language remain the barrier
that keeps her here. Next thing,
the phone comes out and you walk on ahead.

Sorting out plans for the weekend
you choose a foreign tongue: *Cherpsing,
guaning, reem, butters, neek, peng and chung.*

The Disinclination

Outside, a swirling raggle-taggle of snowflakes.
This afternoon the garden will pretend to be the South Pole
but I have no intention of conquering it.

No more than I had the desire last week
to wade shin-deep through a collage of crisp leaves
and kick them back up into the trees.

Nor last month, stoop and snuffle for conkers
adding to my collection of miniature shrunken heads.
The burrs of adolescence finally brushed off.

My wife suggests a bracing walk. I decline.
Instead, to bed with a book and what's left of the wine.

Wobblies

Invited to the launch of a book entitled
A Handy Guide for Grandparents,
in the spirit of caricature I dressed
as a cartoon grandfather.

Collarless shirt with braces and muffler,
baggy grey cardigan and woolly mittens,
wire specs, flat cap and smelly old pipe.
But nobody noticed.

My embarrassment turned to anger.
'I'm exposing stereotypes,' I shouted.
'Please raise your glasses and drink
a toast to Irony.'

In the silence that followed I slammed
my glass down on the table, spilling wine
over a stack of signed books. The author
was the first to exit.

I proffered my muffler to the store manager
as she wiped the covers with a tissue.
'No worries,' she whispered. 'In the early stages
my grandad used to throw wobblies like that.
Nice cup of tea?'

What is the word . . .

You turn your chair away.

Why can't you look me straight in the chair?

There is no light at the end of the flannel.

They pop up, words, I grab the nearest.

It said flannel. Would potato have been better?

Your chair tells me I'm growing crazier.

Flannel, chair, potato, words.

What is the word for . . .

A Cold Calling

Writing a poem was easy. Just pick up the phone,
dial your number and you would be there waiting.
I loved the gift of your gab, funny and unpretentious,
pen in hand, I would get something down every time

If I rang late at night I could tell you'd been drinking
as I tried to unravel the gist of your gabble,
diffuse and surreal. If you were engaged
I would leave a message and you'd return my call

But lately, whenever I remember to ring
the line is invariably busy. When I do get through
your voice sounds cold, distant and indistinct,
as if I were a stranger, just another caller

Between long silences you repeat yourself.
Say the same things over and over. Over and over.
Over and . . .

Thud

I am bereft *thud* of ideas *thud*
No music *thud* in my soul *thud*
The only rhythm *thud* a dull *thud*
Followed by another, *thud* even duller *thud*

'Write a poem about being unable
to write a poem,' you suggest,
trying to be helpful. I try. So far
so good. Then *thud thud thud*.

Barbecuing the Decade

The decade in front of me
is red, brown, red, blue, maroon,
red, blue, red, blue, maroon.

Three thousand six hundred and fifty pages
of days spent. Some well, some half recalled,
most forgotten. The ten on the three-score.

A writer's day-to-day. Appointments
and failed resolutions. Rhymes-in-waiting.
Each year a shadow of the one before.

A typical earthworm will have five hearts
The chance of being struck by lightning is 1 in 3 million
Horses cannot breathe through their mouths.

Ash Wednesday is the time for purification,
for lighting the barbecue, and inviting round
neighbours who have suffered a recent loss.

Into the flames goes the Millennium
followed by brown, red, blue, maroon, etc.
The past crackles like stars. The days curl up and die.

The decade in front of me, an empty shelf.

'Coach & Horses. Interior'

(*After a photograph by Andrew Thorpe*)

What we see in the photograph
taken late in the afternoon
is the corner of an empty bar
and his favourite table

On it stand two pint glasses
and an ashtray in which a cigarette
still burns. The beer is unfinished
as if the drinkers had left in a hurry

What we do not see are the regulars
silent on the pavement in funeral best
Sholto, Don, John, Terry and the rest.
Waving goodbye to Andrew. To each other.

Tomatoes

Out on the sunny patio, the Gro-bag.
Scattered on the compost, your ashes

Come spring, young shoots will rise
and the fruit, like church bells

ring from the vines. Tomatoes,
if not with the taste of you in them

at least, ripening with the memory.

Knock Knock

Who's that at the door
Did I hear someone knock?

It's the man from the volcano
Bearing ash and molten rock

The man from the earthquake
The man from the tsunami

The man from the Taliban
With IEDs for the army

Who's that at the door
Is there someone outside?

It's the man from the cancer
In search of a bride

The man from the kidnap
The man from the abuse

The man from the murder
Still on the loose

The man from the nightmare
The man from the fear

The man from the news
We don't wish to hear

The man with the plans
For the next civil war

Did I hear someone knock
Who's that at the door?

Deadpan Delivery

I was popping a few frozen
fugu fish fingers under the grill
when there came a loud knocking.

Quickly donning my clown costume
I opened the door.
It was the Deadpan Man with a delivery.

'Have I got to sign for this?' I asked.
'No, I'm not hard of hearing,'
he quipped, deadpan.

Indefinite Definitions

ARDVARK

A ardvark is a pig who lives on the veldt
Alphabetically prized and often misspelt

BRUPT

A brupt is a person, curt and impolite
Brusque and impatient
Who thinks he's always right

A cut-you-off-in-conversation
Interrupting sort
And short

BYSMAL

A bysmal I would never befriend
Bonkers, the pits, completely round the bend

CUTE

A cute is sharp, knows all the angles
When it suits, is eager to please
In a tight corner, no angel
Will squeeze you, this one, by degrees

DONIS

A donis thinks he's a hulk
Laugh at his bulk, and he'll sulk

DRENALINE

A drenaline will surprise you
Buck you up and energize you
Faced with a xeman or a grizzly bear
It's handy to have a drenaline there

DRIFT

A drift will often lead you astray
Misdirected you lose your way
End up in a place you'd rather not be
Like the midst of a dark, unwelcoming sea

ECDOTE

An ecdote will make 'em laugh
Especially one about you
Therefore it has to be funny
Although not necessarily true

FICIONADO

A ficionado is a *fan* in Spanish
Loud, intolerant and clannish
And bullfighting he's no wish to banish

GHAST

A ghast is a creature
Who takes a mean delight
In creeping up on children
And giving them a fright

HEM

A hem, kindly take note
Is a clearing, not in the forest
But in the throat

ITCH

A itch is not the tickle
That you scratch until it's stopped
But the sound of an 'h'
(Which should never be dropped)

JAR

A jar enjoys teasing the cat
By leaving a door half open
A childish game.
Draught in the living room?
Cat gets the blame

KIMBO

A kimbo stands, hands on hips
Rattlesnake eyes, smile on lips

Across the open grave of his shadow
You face the sun
Waiting for the sling
Of the kimbo's gun

LERT

A lert sits up straight in class
And pays attention
Lerts are never late for school
Or get detention

MENDS

A mends is what you make
When in a certain mood
Contrite perhaps
After being rather rude

NAGRAM

A nagram is an anagram
Of a granma

ORTA

A orta is not a killer whale
(That's orca), but a large vein
That helps the heart tick

(Orcas in the main
Live in the Arctic)

PHID

A phid is an insect
That sucks juices from plants
Which is why it is foolish
To grow fuchsias in your pants

PLOMB

A plomb is someone
Who is very self-possessed
Downright upright
He thinks that he's the best

A stickler for detail
And tight as a drum
Certain plombs, I have to say
Are a pain in the b*m

POPLEXY

A poplexy is what happens to people
When they get into a rage
It makes them go all purple
And look three times their age

QUATIC

A quatic is quicksilver in water
Without question, quintessentially neat
Except for the propeller-shaped toes
Which make for a strange quirk of feet

RACHNID

A rachnid will elicit night sweats
And bed-quaking screams
When it does a soft-shoe scuttle
Across the floor of your dreams

SH

A sh is very quiet
(Hold your breath)
Ghostly reminder
Of how things were
(And will be)

SKEW

A skew is a seabird
With wings of different sizes
So that when it tries to float
It invariably capsizes

SPARAGUS

A sparagus is nice for tea
Plural, not sparaguses—sparagi

STERISK

A sterisk is a star
Demanding attention
Replacing letters
In words we daren't mention
(Like b*m, for instance)

TOMIC

A tomic is extremely small
But splittable
Economic, but not at all
Hospitable

TONE

A tone puts patience to the test
Says sorry, weeps and beats its breast
Kneels, grovels and rolls on the ground
The tone of a tone is a wailing sound

TROPHY

A trophy not to my taste
Is the one you are given
When shriven
Going to waste

USSIE

A ussie lives downunder
And can be aggressive
No wonder . . .

Ussie males are hard as nails
And think Oz is blessed.
Not to argue, I find best

VOID

A void, if I see, smell or hear of
I tend to keep well clear of

WKWARD

A wkward is an ugly word
And difficult to spell
Ungainly and inelegant
And yet comical as well

XEMAN

A xeman was an expert at decapitating
Seldom kept kings or princesses waiting

Now having lost the taste for blood
Consoles himself by chopping wood

YATOLLAH

A yatollah is a leader
A devout religious man
Who wears a higher collar
If he lives outside Iran

ZURE

A zure is a colour
As blue as blue can be
Blowing kisses from the sky
And on sunny days, the sea

As Far As I Know

As far as I know
I have never received a bribe, fiddled my expenses
or hacked into anybody's voicemail

As far as I can be sure
I have never broken into a stranger's home,
stolen valuables, and then trashed the place

I am pretty certain
I have never knowingly molested a woman
walking home alone after dark

I would remember surely
if I had pushed excrement, or worse still,
a lighted rag soaked in paraffin
through a neighbour's letter-box

To the best of my knowledge
I have never jumped the queue at the Post Office,
or taken a baseball bat to a former accomplice

Correct me if I am wrong
but I have never planted a bomb under a stationary car
without the owner's consent

I think I can safely say
in fact, I'm pretty sure, that I have never
smuggled heroin into this country
from places like overseas

As far as I know
I have never received stolen excrement
Pushed heroin through a neighbour's letter-box
Taken an overseas woman at the Post Office
Smuggled bribes, fiddles or paraffin
Planted stationery or valuable rags after dark
Hacked into a lighted car with a baseball bat
Or molested a bomb soaked in voicemail.

As far as I know

Beyond Compare

Dearest, do not mourn for me overlong,
Christina and Dylan had it right
When soon I have done with raging
and gone gentle into that good night

To help you negotiate the grief
a few guidelines on how to behave
During the half-life that awaits you
when I am dead in the grave

For you to find another leading man
would not be unreasonable, given your age
An understudy who has been biding his time
learning my lines below stage

But don't be rushed. Should he move in
take your time and find the space
To enlighten this johnny-come-lately
so that from the start he knows his place

Put our wedding portrait on the bedside table
but don't make of it a shrine. Rugby shield
and team photos on the piano. Tennis cups?
One of our mixed doubles would be fine.

Write down my quips and anecdotes
learned by heart, they'll prove useful one day
When, in company, his attempts at humour
you can top with 'Or, as Geoffrey used to say . . .'

Doubtless sex will be part of the equation
but don't encourage him, that wouldn't be fair
And let it be known after he's tried it on
that your previous was beyond compare

If he needs a holiday insist on Spain
our favourite hotel in that glorious location
Where, among our old friends around the pool
you can sprinkle me into the conversation

And on the balcony one evening,
when the sun, like a penny, finally drops into the sea
He might feel a chill, touch your arm,
and wish to god he'd been me.

Johnny-Come-Lately

Such fortunate timing! No, not your dying
but my receiving your letter on the very morning
I intended posting mine.

Imagine your embarrassment, not to say shock
at reading my farewell letter on your deathbed.
You had enough to contend with surely.

I had no idea you were fatally ill,
you should have said. Had I known,
I would have cancelled my 'business trip'.

The plan was that I would join John in Brussels
and send it from there. Better, we thought,
than risking a dreadful scene in Finchley.

We had kept our affair secret for years.
But with the children having flown the coop
decided it was time to make a clean break.

Having been through one messy divorce,
John (or 'Johnny-come-lately', life imitating Art!)
will be relieved at not having to face another.

Now of course everything is on hold
until the end of the year. Time for the widow
to put on a show of grief before moving on.

Sell the house and dispose of the contents.
Good riddance! (No, not you, Geoffrey,
I mean the clutter that clings to one over the years.)

And it's adios to that poncey hotel in Pollensa
and those pompous pricks around the pool.
John has a cottage in Provence. Bliss!

Re: sex, too late now not to encourage him
and to make comparisons wouldn't be fair
But comparatively speaking, I fear you don't compare.

Your quips and anecdotes? In one ear and out the other.
But you're right about Rossetti and that line from a Dylan song,
Worry not, my dearest, I shall not mourn overlong.

The Publicist's Last Letter

Tell them I was happy
That despite the chemo and hair-loss
I kept on smiling. That I was brave.

Tell them I was cracking jokes
right up to the end.
Please forward my last words asap.

Tell them the funeral was a triumph
with nationwide coverage
and moving tributes from all my slebs.

Tell them my phone
is in the casket fully charged
should heaven require my services

Tell them I made my peace with god.
Tell me, is there one?
Tell me, was I happy?

At Home with the Surrealists

Mrs Magritte

René is becoming insufferable, sucking on his pipe
like a baby on its sucette, even during supper. Last night
everybody around the table was coughing as the room
filled with the smoke of his foul-smelling tobacco.

When at last I remonstrated, he smirked and said
'Ceci n'est pas une pipe.' Picking up the soup ladle
I replied artfully, 'Et ceci n'est pas une louche,'
before thwacking him soundly on the side of the head.

Mrs Duchamp

I am becoming increasingly worried about Marcel's drinking.
Since coming to New York he spends his nights in seedy bars
on the Lower East Side, coming home the worse for wear.

Only this morning I found him slumped on the landing
his arms around a gentleman's urinal. On sobering up
his excuses were readymade. He was minding it for a friend.

He won it in a raffle. Being thirsty he had mistaken it for a fountain.
Eventually, after much nagging, he dragged it down stairs
and dumped it on the steps of an art gallery two blocks away.

Mrs Dali

I was in the kitchen wondering what to cook for supper
When Salvador telephoned to confess he had taken a lover.
How typical of him not to have the courage to tell me
face to face. Nor even take the time to compose a letter.

Angrily I tossed the handset into a pan of boiling water
and ate it later with boiled potatoes and a fresh green salad.

Mrs Ray

Man turned up
out of the blue

'Un cadeau
just for you

A peace offering,'
he said

I forgave him
we went to bed

After he'd gone
I heated it on the stove

Ironed his shirts
vests, pants

All ripped to shreds
Our love.

Fizzing in Chiswick

Let's put it down to the drink, but there we were
on the first-floor landing, early evening
and the late sun streaming through the study window

Downstairs the party was in two minds,
people still arriving, others shouting noisy farewells.
The popping of corks, the slamming of car doors

It was your voice that drew me up the stairs,
the eyes that kept me there, and then the arms.
Half your age, I was flattered by the attention

Though still a beauty, there was desperation
about your flirting, an only-child-like clinging
that gave off the stale musk of loneliness

Was I to be the last fling of the dice
before the corks finally stopped popping
and the evening slammed shut like a car door?

When I admitted to not knowing who you were,
nor having heard, never mind read, any of your books,
you froze before melting away in search of more fizz

Hours later, embarrassed but still captivated
I sought you out. Found you in the darkness
of my father's study, the two of you, fizzing.

'And when did you last see your father?'

(William Frederick Yeames, 1878)

'And when did you last see your father?'
'Never.' The officer leaned forward bemused:
'Don't get all Cavalier with me
We Roundheads are not easily amused.

Time is of the essence, so answer me quick
Or it's over the table and out with the stick.
When did you last see your father? I repeat.'
The boy mumbled, now white as a sheet.

'A soldier, he disappeared before I was born
Leaving my mother and sister forlorn
For I am a bastard, sir, and I carry the shame.'
'Your father's the bastard, now tell me his name.'

The boy went silent, recalling the name of him
'Er . . . Cromwell . . . Oliver, do you know what became of him?'

Spring Resprung

Spring graced us for a day last week,
but despite our warm welcome didn't linger.
Skies clouded over, chill winds resumed
their call to duty, daffodils shivered
and bluebells, miffed, lowered their gaze.

But today it was back, unapologetic,
recharged and full of the joys of giving.
Summer in the offing, life for living.

Vow

I vow to honour the commitment made this day
Which, unlike the flowers and the cake
Will not wither or decay. A promise, not to obey
But to respond joyfully, to forgive and to console,
For once incomplete, we now are whole.

I vow to bear in mind that if, at times,
Things seem to go from bad to worse
They also go from bad to better.
The lost purse is handed in, the letter
Contains wonderful news. Trains run on time,
Hurricanes run out of breath, floods subside,
And toast lands jam-side up.

And with this ring, my final vow:
To recall, whatever the future may bring,
The love I feel for you now.

Tube Strike Haiku

trains that are side-lined
idling in rusty sidings
fear the knacker's yard

tunnels empty now
can see the light at both ends
birds risk a short cut

rails sleeping, dream of
a parallel universe
a new perspective

platforms yawn and stretch
enjoying the holiday
mice minding the gap

Poem on the Underground

$$\text{tu} \qquad \text{be}$$

$$\text{or} \qquad \text{not}$$

$$\text{tu} \qquad \text{be}$$

Concourse

Lonely on a crowded concourse?
Don't grow cantankerous
Somebody loves you
Here at St Pancras.

The Waiting Game

Love can sweeten the waiting game.
When I look at the destination board
in the hope of seeing your name.
When I listen to announcements
of delays, or a cancelled train
in the hope of hearing you mentioned,
sadly, always in vain. On every screen
and hoarding do I see your face?
Like the lovers in the statue
do we melt in eternal embrace?
The ticket from the Fast Machine
will your name be printed on it?
On the back of every Freedom Pass
in praise of you, a sonnet.

Ode to the Leaf

(Nissan's zero-emission electric car)

Cornering too fast
He came to grief
Spun out of control
Turned over a new Leaf.

Relief All Round

After the Poetry Society AGM
as people filed out into the street

A sniper opened fire
from a rooftop opposite.

Luckily,
there were no bards holed.

Nice Try

You say if we hid under bushes
or darted from shade to shade
then we might get by unnoticed.

Unlikely. We are vastly outnumbered.
As we speak, they're out there
scythes at the ready, playing hide and seek.

Me under a bush, you in the shade
someone counting to ten, sharpening a blade.

Font

bequeathed a font,
a modest typeface,
my dna selected lowercase

i'd have preferred something
to make the page sit up
and the reader take notice

of course, it's what you say,
not how you look. but now i'm older
i wish my genes had gone for something

b o l d e r

To Roget's Thesaurus

Don't worry, Roget, I won't play that silly game
diversion, entertainment, distraction, sport, pastime

Of writing down a list of words
terms, utterances, vocables, parts of speech

To celebrate what a godsend you are. Honest!
True, frank, candid, sincere, simple, veracious, guileless, warts and all.

Another Person's Dog

No, not yours. Yours is lovely.
It's another person's dog.

the mean snapper
the whiskery whirlwind
the farter and snarler
the piddler and dribbler
the shedder of hairs
the sniffer of arses
the prowler growling
at anything that passes
the bellicose paws,
the yellowing claws

No, not yours. Yours is lovely.

I wish I could be kinder
But this is how it ends
To write about another person's dog
And lose all your friends.

Father's American Walking Sticks

Whereas some men in the neighbourhood kept pigeons,
Dad kept *phasmids*. Easy to breed, the nymphs
being parthenogenetic, he kept them in a shed in the back yard.

As a postman, he finished work early, leaving his afternoons
free to pursue his hobby. He had hundreds,
all stick-shapes and sizes, and he knew many by name.

Meera, Kalpana, Yasmin were his favourite *Common Indians*,
Betty and Bud the *American Walking Sticks* he handled with care,
Cyclops, the three-legged *Giant Spiny*, Zaza the *Praying Mantis*.

We spent hours in the shed, him waxing lyrical about compost,
me desperate for a skirmish or a coupling, even a twitch,
so I was delighted when mother brought home a puppy.

Monty was a fully grown Welsh collie when Dad died,
and suddenly our walks by the river became dismal affairs.
Until, that is, I remembered the phantoms in the shed.

Careful not to mix the species, I took a handful every day
and on reaching a quiet spot, and in memory of my father,
I would throw a stick insect for Monty to fetch.

Confused by camouflage, he rarely brought one back,
but he enjoyed the chase, racing across an open field
like a black and white flag unfurling in the wind.

It was a *Walking Stick*, Betty, if I'm not mistaken,
who sprayed him in the eyes as he tried to retrieve her,
putting a painful stop to our playful memento mori.

So, heavy of heart, I emptied the shed, loaded the car,
and resisting the temptation to play Poohsticks,
drove into the countryside, where I set them free.

At 3 a.m. I awake with a start. The sound of a branch
tapping at the bedroom window. It grows louder.
But there is no wind, no tree, no garden. Louder.

Events & Happenings 1964

It began like any other, trying to draw attention to itself.
Jumping up and down, 'Look at me, look at me.'
But once the smoke had cleared, bells fallen silent
and auld acquaintances forgot, what do I remember
of sixty-four? Race riots, the jailing of Mandela,
Vietnam, Harold Wilson, the last hanging in Britain,
the Beatles, and of course, finding you.

Liverpool 8

Evenings we'd spend together in the cellar bar below
Venture upstairs occasionally to watch a theatre show
Events and Happenings, poems on Monday nights
Read by wistful beatniks fed on City Lights
Young, we talked of freedom, pop art, CND,
Miniskirts and football, and we danced to R&B,
At midnight we'd wander home with dreams enough to spare
Now I wander still down Hope Street but you're no longer there.

Liverpool 9

While we sleep, heads in the clouds, who drops kicking into history?
A quarrel over money, murder, a medallion left at the scene.
Local girl Norma points the finger at Peter and Gwynne. Sorry, lads.
Two trapdoors open for the last time with macabre synchronicity.
On the other side of the East Lancs, a mirror image. Strangeways.
No dreams to spare. Nightmare, a tumbril's ride from Hope Street.

To Macca's Shirt

(On exhibition at the Museum of Liverpool, alongside Macca's trousers)

You arrived washed, ironed and lightly starched.
Stars and stripes on the label, *'Broadway and Sunset Strip'*
Assumed he'd brought you back from his first American trip.

But you weren't my style. Too flash for a teacher
I left you in the laundry bag and squirrelled you away.
Forty years on I re-read the label: *Esquire regd. Glasgow.*

May 1960, the Silver Beatles on tour with Johnny Gentle.
Two weeks in Scotland, bread on the night, and the lure
of the Sanforized shrunk imports in the Esquire shop.

Though never quite living up to the promise of your name,
at least you appeared on stage and realized your dreams.
Felt a sense of history coursing through your seams.

The alternative? Shoplifted by a teddy boy from Alloa
for the dance at the Town Hall. Lipstick on your collar,
sweat on your oxters and blood on your cuffs.

To end up here, the carapace of a silver beetle,
pinned down under glass, would have been unthinkable.
A shroud, ghostly, Sanforized and unshrinkable.

Home Truths

Nine thirty-five one Saturday morning in Liverpool
and the restaurant at the Adelphi Hotel is heaving.
The only man not wearing a track suit has just entered
and stands confused by the panoply of muscle and Lycra,
the smell of liniment and deep-fried potato nuggets.

A waitress, recognizing John Peel, leads him to a table
in the corner and explains, 'It's bedlam in here today.
Amateur boxers from all over the world.' Once seated,
she whispers, 'It's self-service too, but I'm a huge fan
so what can I get yer?' John confides in the name-tag

'To be honest, Susan, I can't be doing with all that fried stuff,
what I'd really like is a couple of lightly poached eggs on toast.'
Susan nods 'Very wise, very wise.' She looks at him proudly.
'I suppose you're back home for the big game at Anfield?
It's good to see you haven't grown too big for your roots.'

Relaxed now, John weighs up the flies and feathers,
bantams and welters, middles and heavies.
Picks out a seven-stone Cuban and climbs into the ring.
On the count of ten, Susan returns empty-handed.
'Sorry, John, Chef can't be arsed.'

Scorpio

'Fearless, intense, secretive and vengeful,
passionate, lusty in the extreme', this Scorpio
acknowledges the characteristics ascribed
to his zodiac sign. Except for revenge.
This Scorpio does not have a sting in its tail.

Unlike Lancashire hotpot, revenge is a dish
best served cold, in this case a paperweight.
A dome of solid glass containing a scorpion
with a tail like a malevolent question mark.
A souvenir from a trip to New Mexico.

I will never reveal the names of those strangers,
fellow poets some of them, and literary critics
who have made public fools of my children.
They know who they are. Those still alive, that is.
Their names inscribed on the base of a paperweight.

Eleven in all. A few critics still making a living
as nightwatchmen in cemeteries, some poets
have won prizes, others, deserted by the muse,
no longer published. Whenever we meet
I play the innocent, accept their faux-bonhomie.

Only one is a woman. A poet whose photograph
never appears on the back cover of her books.
And on meeting her recently for the first time
I could understand why, and it cheered me no end.
But fleetingly, for she is old now, and semi-retired.

Some may even regret their youthful bile,
their mistrust of popular culture, and the working class.
This is just to let them know, that though forgiven,
they are not forgotten, their names weighted down
beneath a scorpion preserved in glass.

Not for Me a Youngman's Death

Not for me a youngman's death
Not a car crash, whiplash
John Doe at A&E kind of death.
Not a gun in hand, in a far-off land
IED at the roadside, death

Not a slow-fade, razor blade
bloodbath in the bath, death.
Jump under a train, Kurt Cobain
bullet in the brain, death

Not a horse-riding, paragliding
mountain climbing fall, death.
Motorcycle into an old stone wall
you know the kind of death, death

My nights are rarely unruly.
My days of all-night parties
are over, well and truly.
No mistresses no red sports cars
no shady deals no gangland bars
no drugs no fags no rock 'n' roll
Time alone has taken its toll

Let me die an oldman's death
Not a domestic brawl, blood in the hall
knife in the chest, death.
Not a drunken binge, dirty syringe
'What a waste of a life', death.

Why Me?

'Why me?' They question, and rightly so.
Why them? An early death, an unexpected blow.

But when three score and ten has been achieved,
the boxes ticked, it's reassuring the bereaved

Won't wring their hands, look heavenwards and cry
'Life's so unfair, he was too young to die.'

'Why me? Why me?' The strangled prayer.
The simple answer, 'Because you're there.'

Hill o' Beans

'Life ain't nuttin' but a hill o' beans,' drawled Granma.
And removing her corn cob pipe
spat a stream of baccy juice into the empty firegrate,
before settling back with a jug of bourbon
into her old rockin' chair.

To think,
only this time last year
she was working for the Welsh Water Authority.

Grandma and the Angels

Whenever it snowed
Grandma would say
'The angels are having a pillow-fight'

Whenever thunder rumbled
She would say
'The angels are rearranging the furniture'

Whenever gales rattled the windows
Grandma would say
'The angels are blowing on their hot soup'

Whenever someone died
She would say
'The angels have a new friend to play with'

When Grandma passed away
So did the angels.

A Good Age

On reaching a good age
she died

The years before
had all been bad

Then she reached a good age
and died. How sad. How sad.

'Look, Daddy, the Candle is Crying'

Is it, my dear?
And are they tears of joy for the birthday boy
hunched above the cake, impatient for the count of three?

Or tears of sadness
at the thought of its journey into darkness,
ending with a hiss of smoke in a puddle of grease?

No, the candle is not crying.
The heat of the flame generated by the wick
absorbs the liquid and pulls it upward where it is vaporized.
What you mistake for tears are merely droplets of melting
    paraffin wax.
Now off to bed you go, and stop being silly.

And So to Bed

Bed of roses
Once is enough

Bed of nails
Hot-water bottle
out of the question

Bed of contention
Some nights
its snoring
keeps me awake

Cricket bed
A drive
into the covers

Sea bed
A dive
into the billows

Torre del Lago bed
On the wall
photographs of Puccini
On the ceiling
quavers, dots and minims
A jarring discord of mosquitoes

Nostalgia bed
How I miss
Momma's
apple-pie beds

Death Row bed
The electric blanket
is still used in Nebraska
Tennessee and Alabama

Strange bed
Who is this stranger?
What is she doing?

Philosophical bed
In pursuit of wisdom
T. E. Lawrence
slept on seven pillows

Amsterdam bed
After John and Yoko
It became unbearable

Sleepy bed
Do Not Disturb
The sign on the door
of the hotel room.
The bed is asleep

Strange bedfellows
Marcel Proust and Eric Cantona

Quisling bed
In bed with the enemy.
It was hopeless.
The goose-stepping
The endless 'Heil Hitler!'s

Unmade bed
Among cardboard and polythene,
cam dowels and barrel nuts,
tear-stained diagrams for flatpack
self-assembly, the suicide note

Paranoid bed
Ghosts of ducks
long since plucked
waddle menacingly
across the eiderdown

Luton, Beds., bed
That flat in Luton
Slept on a futon
With my suit on

Brothel bed
Can't bear to look at itself
in the overhead mirror

Camp bed
A la Recherche du Temps Perdu
on the bedside table
Gardenia on the pillow
Silk pyjamas neatly folded

Sick bed
Open windows
and remove bedding.
Scrub with disinfectant

Hospital bed
What it becomes
if the above is ignored

Death bed
Who knows?
You may be lying in it

Strange bedfellows
Goldilocks and W. H. Auden

Bed possessed by evil spirits
Send for a priest
Exorcism the remedy.
Failing that, the Beast.
Invoke Baron Samedi

Dog on the bed
'Whose dog is that?'

Pirate bed
Parrot on the headboard
Peg-leg on the floor
Cutlass hanging from the hook
embedded in the door

Bed on fire
Yesterday the smoke alarm
burst into flames,
and now this

Strange bedfellows
Hitler and Yoko Ono

Put-u-up beds
Get-u-up early
in the morning

Truckle-beds
Commercially,
Four-poster truckle-beds
never caught on

Twin beds
Ideal for twins

Islamabed
Facing towards Mecca

Papal bed
Holier than thine

Queen-sized bed
Bags of room
for Her Majesty
to reign over us

Get-out-of-beds
Beds do not
have wrong sides

Strange bedfellows
Baron Samedi and Pooh Bear

And so to bed.

Acknowledgements

'Nice Try' was originally published in *Poetry Review*. 'Events & Happenings 1964' appears in *Jubilee Lines* (Faber and Faber). This collection contains revised versions of 'Deadpan Delivery', 'Hill o' Beans' and 'Indefinite Definitions', first published in *Lucky* (Viking). The author wishes to acknowledge Kenneth Koch as the source of inspiration for 'And So to Bed'.